RAINBOWS
All Around

Suzanne Hardin

illustrated by Marjorie Scott

Learning Media

1.
On the Bus

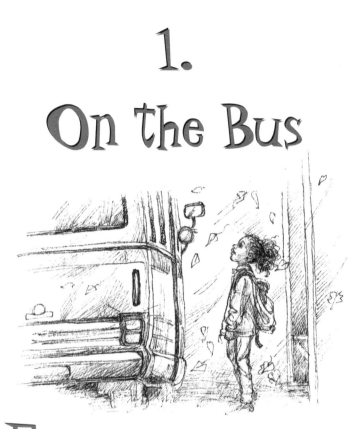

Fall leaves floated down like snowflakes as Bailey waited at the bus stop. Soon the bus pulled up, with its flashing red lights and squeaky brakes. The driver slid the door open, and Bailey jumped on board.

She pulled off her backpack and flopped into a seat as the bus rumbled on its way.

"Hi, Elena," she called out to a classmate.

Elena sat across the way in a flood of morning sunlight. Bailey saw the string of bright beads around her neck.

"Where did you get the cool necklace?" she asked.

"Kaytlin made it for me," said Elena. "We've got a club. All four of us have these necklaces."

Bailey loved to make things. She wanted to look at the necklace up close, but Elena turned and stared out the window until the bus reached the school gates.

2.

The Club

At recess, Bailey saw Elena and the other girls huddled together on the playground. They were looking at each other's necklaces and talking about names for their club.

"I think we should call our club The Flamingoes," she heard Kaytlin say to the others. "I've seen them down in Florida. They're the same color as these bright pink beads."

"How about The Mermaids?" suggested Elena. "These blue beads look like the sea."

Then all four girls seemed to be talking at once. They sounded like bees buzzing in a hive. But when Bailey walked up to them, the group grew silent.

"How did you make the neat necklaces, Kaytlin?" Bailey asked.

The small knot of girls looked up at Bailey, but no one answered. They stared at her for a moment and then looked at Kaytlin.

"Sorry, Bailey, they're just for our club,"
Kaytlin said, and the four friends went
to sit over by the drinking fountains.

Bailey spent the rest of the recess alone
at the swings.

3.

Friday Night

When Bailey's mom went out to work on Friday night, Erika came to look after her. Erika was in high school. She lived just down the street, and Bailey always looked forward to seeing her. They *always* had fun together.

They played cards for a while, and then Erika braided Bailey's hair.
She tried a new style every time she came over.

"Supper time," said Erika. "I could eat a horse! Let's see what we can find in the pantry."

As they fixed sandwiches, Bailey saw a flash of color on Erika's ankle. It was some kind of bracelet.

"Where did you get that, Erika?" Bailey asked.

"I made it," Erika said. "It's called a friendship bracelet. Would you like to make one for yourself?"

"Could I?" Bailey's eyes grew wide. "It looks kind of hard."

"No, it's really easy. Do you have any yarn?" asked Erika.

"I think so. I'll go and look," said Bailey. She left the room and came back with a basket on her arm. She reached in and pulled out a bundle of yarn.

"How's this?" she asked. The yarn was all mixed up, like a fuzzy rainbow.

"Great!" said Erika. "Lots of lovely colors."

Bailey handed the yarn to Erika, and they sat down together on the couch.

4.

Something New

"First you make a loop like this." Erika twisted the yarn into the shape of a teardrop. "Then pull the thread through until it's tight."

Erika leaned closer to Bailey and carefully showed her what to do. "Good. Now grab more thread and pull it through."

Bailey did this a few more times, and soon she could see a pattern.

"That's right. See how easy it is?"

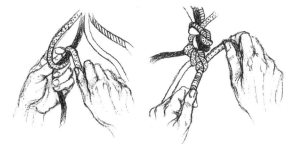

Erika smiled as Bailey worked away. Bailey caught on quickly. It wasn't long before the bracelet was finished.

"Nice job," Erika said as she tied the bright circle of color around Bailey's wrist.

By bedtime, Bailey had made three more bracelets. She looped them round her fingers and held them in her hand while she and Erika read a book together.

When Erika went downstairs, Bailey put the bracelets on the nightstand and turned out the light.

5.

Decisions

As Bailey lay awake in bed, she began thinking about the bracelets.

"I could give the three bracelets to some friends and start my own club," she said to herself.

She thought about which of her classmates she could ask to join her club. It was hard to decide. Some kids would be left out.

Bailey nestled down in her soft bed.
Moonlight was shining through the small
curved window in the corner of her
room. It seemed to cast a spotlight on
the three small bracelets by her bed. She
picked one up and gently ran her fingers
over the soft yarn. Then she fell asleep.

When Bailey woke up the next morning, the bracelet was still in her hand. She put it on the nightstand with the others. She thought about how much fun it had been to make the bracelets, and an idea came to her. She hopped out of bed in a flash. Bailey knew just what she wanted to do.

For the rest of that weekend, Bailey spent every free moment working with the yarn. She worked in the car on the way to her soccer game. She worked at the kitchen table after she had raked the leaves. She worked in her bedroom on Sunday evening after she had finished her homework. Finally, everything was ready.

6.

Back at School

On Monday morning, Bailey stuffed a puffy paper sack into her backpack as she got ready for school. She winked at her mom and headed out the door on her way to the bus stop. It was a cold, blustery morning, but Bailey didn't seem to mind.

At school, she hung the backpack on a hook and took off her coat. Some of her classmates gathered around her. They had seen her bracelet.

"That's neat!" said Keisha.

"Where'd you get it?" asked Jamal.

"I made it," Bailey said as she hung her coat on top of her backpack.

"Can I see it?" asked Carly.

Bailey held out her arm so Carly could examine the bracelet.

Jamal bent down for a closer look. "Was it hard to make?" he asked.

"Not really," Bailey replied.

She was glad her friends liked it. Her lips curled up in a little half-moon smile.

7.

Recess

At recess, Kaytlin came up to Bailey in the playground while she was jumping rope with some other kids.

"Will you show me how to make one of those bracelets?" she asked.

Bailey was surprised that Kaytlin had spoken to her. She looked at the gleaming beads on Kaytlin's necklace.

Bailey thought for a moment. Then she said, "Sure. I'll bring some yarn and show you tomorrow."

Kaytlin smiled and ran back to join her friends.

Bailey stood silently, watching her classmates. Some were playing basketball, some were climbing the Eagle's Perch, and others were swinging on the swings.

Then someone called out to her,
"C'mon! It's your turn, Bailey!"

Bailey heard the steady tap of the rope
as it touched the ground. She waited for
a second or two, and then she darted in
and began to jump.

8.
Sharing Time

At the end of the day, Bailey's teacher, Mr. Arata, called the class up to the front of the room for sharing circle.

Reed talked about his new chameleon. Every eye was on the little animal as its color changed from bright green to a dull brown.

Melissa showed the class the remote control car she had gotten for her birthday.

Bailey was the last one to share. When it was her turn, she brought out her lumpy paper sack.

"I have something to pass out to the class," she told Mr. Arata.

"Fine," he said. "Go ahead, Bailey."

Bailey moved around the circle, giving everyone a bracelet made from colorful twists of yarn. She and her classmates helped each other tie them on. There was even one for Mr. Arata.

When she had finished, she looked up.
She was sure that nobody was feeling left
out that day. Only four children had
bead necklaces, but everyone had a
bracelet. There were smiles and rainbows
all around the room.

Make Your Own Bracelets

You need two pieces of colored wool or thread, each three feet long. Fold them in half and tie a loop knot at the folded end. Stick the loop to a table with tape.

Knot the first thread around the second thread and pull it tight, like this. Do this again. Now, knot the first thread around the third thread in the same way, twice. Do the same thing with the fourth thread. Do this over and over again and watch your bracelet grow.

When your bracelet is long enough, twist each pair of threads together into a strand. Tie a knot in the end of each strand.

Thread one strand through the loop and tie it to the other strand.

If you want to make a wider bracelet, try using six threads instead of four.